A SINGLE MOM'S POST-DIVORCE ROADMAP TO CLOSURE

SIX SIMPLE STEPS FROM PAIN TO POWER

Clairine B. Yomi

Table of Contents

Dedication

To all single moms who step up against all odds to raise their children with poise and dignity.

Acknowledgements

I want to express my deepest gratitude to my entire family, my kids, my parents, my siblings, my nephews, and nieces, our in-laws, for their invaluable support, unwavering love, and encouragement.

Special thanks to:

- Josiane, for her eagle eye as she meticulously scrutinized this book (so, any mistake is my own);

- My beta readers, clients and coachees, for their deep insights and pertinent reviews;

- My Canadian and American Teams for their invaluable feedback and support.

Foreword

I started reading many books on divorce recovery while still facing the pangs and the pains of my divorce, only to abandon them halfway.

Whenever I came across a book, I would be so hopeful that I might have finally found the one that would show me how to let go of practice.

However, these books did a good job explaining that I should let go, why it is important to forgive for my own sake, and that I should move on.

I never finished reading most of them. I was always frustrated because they focused on the outcome, not the healing process.

They were good at the theory and fell short as far as practice was concerned.

I needed to know what I should do in practice, to let go and move on. I needed concrete steps and guidance, not just empty words, clichés, and platitudes.

I wanted to know how to navigate through the pain and find healing.

The books I had come across seemed to miss the mark, leaving me feeling even more lost and frustrated.

As a single mom, I yearned for a resource that would provide me with practical advice and strategies to truly let go and move forward, for myself and for my kids.

This is one of the core reasons why I became a Closure Coach™. Actually, I made that title up, but it encapsulates what I do today.

I wanted to fill the gap that I felt existed in the available resources for divorce recovery.

I wanted to create a guide that would not only explain the importance of letting go and moving on but also provide practical steps and strategies to help other people, and especially single moms, navigate through the healing process.

Becoming a Closure Coach™ was my way of offering the support and guidance that I wished I had found during my own divorce.

This book, the *A Single Moms Roadmap to Closure: Six steps from Pain to Power* is therefore not an academic or a theoretical book.

It is a breakdown of the six steps that fast-tracked my recovery, that I was aware of and that I recognized in hindsight.

In this book, I share my personal journey and the steps that helped me find closure after my divorce.

These steps are not just theoretical, but practical strategies that can be implemented to navigate through the healing process.

My desire is that by the time you close the last pages of this book, you would have achieved three things:

- ✓ positively reframed your experience and your past as steppingstones rather than obstacles.

- ✓ your self-esteem and self-confidence will sky-rocket and you will feel unstoppable.

- ✓ adopted a radically forward-looking attitude that says "Bring it on" to the world.

By sharing my own experiences and providing concrete steps, I hope to offer support and guidance to other single moms, to help them heal and thrive.

I have already shared these simple steps with hundreds of women with exceptionally great results. In fact, many single moms have described this process as a "mindset makeover".

Now is your turn to overhaul your mindset and seize the reins of your destiny,

Clairine B. Yomi
The Closure Coach™

How I Got Here

My divorce was officially granted 17 years ago. We had been separated for three years already, and at the time of separation, we had three kids, and the fourth was on the way.

I left after a violent night, and my Ex said I would "crawl back" to him in no time. He said I would not amount to anything, that my prime had expired, that nobody would want used goods with four kids.

Yes, he had a way with words, and they would cut deep and hurt. I never got used to this in almost 11 years of marriage.

I got married in Cameroon, central Africa at 19. Or should I say given away in marriage? One day, out of the blue, I was told I had a suitor and before I knew it, wedding arrangements were being made.

Within five months, everything was done, and I was now in another family, with people I barely knew.

Before the dust could settle on the "celebrations", my husband told me something I was to remember.

He said he had to make something very clear: my future was in my own hands. When I asked what he meant by that, he said I should not count on him for anything.

He emphasized that whatever I brought into this marriage would be mine, and nothing else.

He kept his word.

I was 19, fresh out of high school. I did not have a job, only my dream of furthering my education in Nigeria, supported by my parents before the suitor entered the scene.

My parents continued to pay my school fees while I was married. My mother continued to send me clothes and to take care of most of my needs, and even my children's, eventually.

Yes, my parents fed and clothed my children too, even taking care of hospital bills.

My father was retired, and my mother sold used clothes. In addition, they had to take care of my seven siblings. They were not exactly an affluent family. I am the eldest.

I hustled quite a bit, selling roasted peanuts, plantain chips, homemade crackers, and the like, to take care of myself and my kids.

My Ex used all kinds of tactics to get me to drop out of school, like refusing to pay my tuition or flipping out the light switch so I could not study because he paid the bills.

He said a clerical job was good enough for me, that I had misplaced ambitions. He would gladly pay for a tailoring apprenticeship, but never my tuition at the university where he taught.

He held a PhD and I, a mere high school graduate, was supposed to know my place.

He was verbally and physically abusive. At the beginning I tried to speak up about the abuse, only to be shut down with statements like "you must endure, or "did you think marriage was easy?"

Besides, over the years, he had carefully crafted the image of a caring but poorly employed son-in-law.

That night, he dropped all pretenses. At the time, I had just started a new job and barely had any savings. He wanted my salary to go into his bank account, and I vehemently refused.

He summoned my parents and started lashing out, saying that they were the ones advising me not to give my salary away to him.

When my mother asked him why he thought they had any say in my management of my finances, he charged at her. My mother's teeth bled from the blows.

I think that is when my family realized that I had been keeping the abuse to myself. In the early days, I talked, but no one believed me.

Even after that violent night, my parents left, not before telling me that marriage was to be endured. I told them that as far as I was concerned, the marriage was over, but they thought it was just an emotional reaction.

After all, I was four months pregnant. Where would I go?

According to my ex, the hardships I would face at my parents' would force me to "crawl back" to him.

I never went back, and ever since I left over twenty years ago, he never held any of his children's hands. He said he would happily watch me suffer because, supposedly, that was "the life I had chosen".

It is ironic that even on this point, we disagreed. He thought a life of abuse under "his roof" was better for me, and I thought my "suffering" outside of that marriage was more bearable than my pseudo-marriage.

So, to punish me, he withdrew his affection and even his presence from his kids. It's been over 20 years, and they have barely seen him for five hours.

And to crown it all, he had my kid's teacher, whom he was already involved with, move in a month after I left.

I cannot explain how utterly gutted and crushed I initially felt.

However, through my journey, I have learned a thing or two, and now, I want to share how, as a newly divorced single mom, you can find closure and move on, for your and your children's sake.

You would agree that raising your children alone, without their father in the picture, after a divorce or separation is not easy.

The pain of divorce is still present, and you are trying to piece your heart back together so you can be emotionally available to your children.

Every day feels like a battle, with the weight of separation hanging heavy on your shoulders.

With conviction, you vow to rise above the pain and be there for your children in all the ways they need most.

However, the path to healing is challenging because you have no idea where to start, you have no idea what to do with your feelings, your anger, your frustration, your bitterness and, quite frankly, your deep desire for revenge.

How many times did you "decide" that you would stop crying?

How many times did you decide never to allow the memories of your life together to resurface and trigger you?

How often did you relapse and cry your heart out, despite your good intentions?

How often did you tell yourself that you were better off, only to break down again?

How many times have you made some resolutions, but your emotions decided to take you on a different path, as if they had a mind of their own?

Well, actually, they do, and the goal of this book is to show you how to get your emotions on your team.

I am a sucker for good and well plotted romance movies. I wish moving on worked just the way they usually describe it in those movies.

Typically, when people experience a breakup, they embark on a journey of self-discovery, seeking healing in various forms. Therapy becomes a haven where they unravel their tangled emotions and learn to forgive themselves and their ex-partner.

They reclaim their identity, and the pieces of their heart slowly start to weave together, transforming from fragments of pain to threads of resilience.

They realize that although divorce may have shattered their world, it has also presented an opportunity to rebuild something stronger and more authentic.

Their children, when they are in the picture, become their guiding lights, reminding them of the love within and around them. Their innocent wisdom teaches them the importance of cherishing the present moment, for healing begins in life's simple joys.

They embark on new adventures with their children, creating beautiful memories that disperse the lingering heaviness of separation. Slowly, their perspective shifts.

The weight on their shoulders no longer feels burdensome but rather a symbol of the strength they have gained.

The pain of divorce is now a thing of the past that no longer defines them. Instead, it becomes a testament to their resilience and a reminder that wounds can be mended, and that "this too shall pass".

They discover the power of self-love and compassion. They embrace the idea of forgiveness, not only towards their ex-partner but also towards themselves.

In time, the pain of divorce becomes a distant memory, one that has shaped them but no longer defines them. They find solace in the love they have rebuilt within their family.

The past is no longer a burden but a steppingstone toward a brighter future.

Lessons emerge, and in the depths of their hearts, they find gratitude for the journey, as it has shaped them into more compassionate and resilient.

Their heart, though once broken, now beats with newfound strength. They are not just emotionally available for their children but for themselves as well.

They eventually find what is then considered true love and go off to live happily ever after, as the credits roll on the screen.

I am sure you must have scoffed many times while reading this inept description of what it feels like to be in pain after a divorce. I have never seen it captured adequately in movies. No words can adequately describe it.

No wonder, for so many women, this journey to healing may take years, double digits of years, as painful memories keep resurfacing, causing waves of grief that consume them.

What if I told you that it does not have to be that way?

What if I told you that you do not need to spend years in grief over your marriage and your EX, whatever the depths of your pain?

What if I told you that you can fast-track your healing if you are committed to applying the steps I will outline for you in this book?

What if I told you there is a way to safely fast-track your healing and bring you to a state where you are ready to live on your own terms and thrive?

What if I told you there are tools to get your emotions, your memories and even your reactions on your team, so that you can live a more satisfactory life?

Yes, divorce will always be a part of your story, but it should not define you. It should not paralyze you. You need to emerge with a heart that is not just pieced back together, but one that is stronger, more resilient, and at peace.

Your journey through life continues. You must embrace the future with open arms, for yourself and for your kids, knowing that your emotional availability will shape their lives for the better.

Healing is a precondition for stepping back into your power. But most single moms don't have a roadmap to follow to achieve peace and closure and step into their power.

This book will provide you with a roadmap to move from pain to power in the shortest time possible. So, hang tight.

Together, we will embark on a transformative journey of healing and empowerment.

First, and foremost, it is essential to acknowledge your pain. Divorce or separation creates a deep wound that can leave you emotionally scarred for life.

If not managed properly, you may grieve for years, even decades, with virtually no prospects of healing. I recently spoke with a single mom who, nine years after her divorce, is still crying as if it happened six months ago.

I know she is not the only one in this situation.

So, in this book, I am offering you a step-by-step process. I have already helped hundreds if not thousands of single moms with, and with amazing results.

I am not saying that you should not grieve. I am saying that if it takes too long, you may miss out on life.

I know a single mom who took seven years to get back on her feet and took five other years in anger over herself for taking so long to realize that she was "wasting her time".

No one can dictate how long someone should grieve. However, if you picked up this book, you are open and ready for closure; that is all that matters.

It is equally important to recognize that seeking help is not a sign of weakness, but rather an act of self-care and empowerment. It takes courage to acknowledge that we need support and to take the necessary steps to seek it.

I know a single mom who did not want anyone to know that she was looking for divorce recovery resources online because, in her words, she needed to "appear strong". She said she would sneak into my Facebook Page often, but she will make sure she never leaves a comment or a "Like", for fear that someone she knows might see it.

Eventually, she realized, after reading one of my posts, that she was only postponing the inevitable, and she was a ticking time bomb, both to herself and her kids.

Unexpressed and unreleased emotions are like a bomb inside a pressure cooker. When it explodes, it can shatter not only the container but also the peace and harmony that once surrounded it, leaving behind a turbulent aftermath of more hurt and chaos.

As you read this book, my first recommendation to you is to be gentle and patient in this process, and do not skip the steps. Granted, some of them overlap, but make sure you follow the process meticulously.

At this point, I also need to be totally transparent with you. The most important ingredient that will fast-track your healing is not in this book, it is in you: Your awareness.

You already made good use of it by picking up this book. Now, I will invite you to focus on the content, and do the exercises offered for the best results.

This entire book is an exercise in sharpening your awareness and raising your consciousness to help you regain your confidence, your self-esteem, and rebuild your life.

By the time you finish reading the Roadmap to Closure, and implementing the steps outlined here, you will feel ignited to thrive and you will be confident about your future.

You will feel unstoppable.

However, we will start with a test to gauge where you are emotionally and establish a baseline.

Time Does Not Heal

My heart breaks every single time I read a message from a single mom sharing how much she is in pain ever since her relationship broke up.

Some single moms tell me it's been 2 years, five years, even 10 years, they have not been able to get rid of that heartache, and most importantly, they have not been able to feel confident again as women.

This is a very common problem, and while it is okay to take the time to grieve your relationship, the longer you stay in grief, the harder it will be for you to break free.

This problem is also common because of the erroneous belief that "time heals all wounds".

Let me share with you one of the core principles of my work as a Closure Coach for single moms: Time does NOT heal. You do.

The belief that "time heals all wounds" is a spell, like many other beliefs.

A spell is a power-full statement that justifies itself time and time again. It is a prophecy. If you knew the power of words, you wouldn't speak or even think idly.

When you say, think or believe that "time heals all wounds", you are doing at least these four things to yourself:

- You are saying that something outside of yourself (aka time, which does not even exist), will heal you.

- You have effectively handed over your power, your will, your destiny to time, which again is only a construct, it does not exist.

- You have decided NOT to take responsibility for your own well-being.

- You are not learning the lesson soon enough to avoid going through the same experience, because the earlier you learn, the better off you are.

You don't have to spend years in pain because of an idea you locked into the recesses of your mind.

I know, people are different, they process pain and hurt differently, but that mostly has to do with the conscious part of our makeup.

The operations of our unconscious selves are the same across the board because we are ONE.

So, when you choose to walk the healing path, it is worth examining your beliefs that may stand in your way, search for the spells you might have cast against yourself in the guise of "comforting" words and expressions.

Do you believe that given a process that works, you can find closure?

If others were able to achieve this, why not you?

The Closure Test™

What does closure feel like?

How would you know you have moved on from your breakup or divorce?

I consider the terms "closure", "letting go," and "taking your power back" as synonyms, and they are better experienced than described.

Let's try an experiment. Continue reading, and you will understand and experience it on a different scale.

I can remember the day I found closure: It was the morning after I read a book that impacted me and changed the direction of my thoughts, my speech, my behavior, my heart, and my entire life.

The day you find closure is the day you absolutely take your power back. Many people can't pinpoint the exact time or day it happened, but for some, like me, it is unforgettable.

Now, something quite embarrassing happened, and I think that is when I experienced what letting go and closure feel like.

After I read that book, I felt so light, calm, settled and relaxed that I had the best sleep ever for the first time after separation and nearly peed on my bed.

This is true. After reading the book that night, I felt like I was floating in the air. A heavy weight had lifted, not just from my shoulder, but from my entire being. I felt certain that my kids and I would be fine; I knew with no doubt that my life was back on track.

Now, notice that I recounted my story of closure, but I withheld one key piece of information from you, and you might have asked "what is the title of this book?"

Now, if you are like me, you want to know the answer to this question; you are now invested.

Authors often do this in their books to keep the suspense and hook you. Your frustration grows the longer you must wait. Pay attention to this feeling of frustration, irritation, and potentially anger.

You don't have control. You are hooked, and you have two choices, either you decide it's not an important piece of information and you smoothly unhook or detach yourself mentally, or you decide that you absolutely need that answer, and you will keep reading until you get it.

How are you feeling? Consider your frustration because someone withheld the title of a book, and your emotions when someone withholds their love.

You are experiencing the contrary of closure, and you will only take your power back, albeit on a microscale, when I reveal the book title to you.

Then, when you finally get it, you will exhale deeply, and with that exhalation, you will have unhooked yourself, you will have found closure, you will have taken your power back.

Now, the same things happen with your feelings after a breakup or divorce. You have lots of questions, and you need answers, but those answers are not always forthcoming.

You can only move on if you decide that the issue is not worth your attention anymore, and mean it, or you stick it out until you find some answers.

In the following chapter, I will reveal the title of this wonderful book, which, by the way, you can get for free.

I will also encourage you not to jump to that chapter yet, especially if you are going to take the Closure Test below. I cannot stress this enough.

The Closure Test aims to help you evaluate your emotional detachment or level of closure and emotional healing. You will measure your progress at the end of the book, but you need a baseline at this stage.

You alone know what you are feeling right now or how painful your experience is, and you are best placed to determine if the pain has reduced over time or not. Closure, therefore, is a subjective concept.

Closure means different things to different people. For some, it might involve complete detachment and emotional distance, while for others, it could entail finding ways to coexist peacefully with memories and emotions linked to the past.

Either way, this assessment is inherently subjective, as it revolves around your emotions and experiences. The journey toward closure after a breakup or a divorce is unique, influenced by factors such as the nature of the relationship, the causes of the divorce, and personal coping mechanisms.

This subjectivity is what makes the Closure Test a valuable tool, as it encourages you to engage with your feelings, memories, thoughts, behaviors, and reactions.

Also, this subjectivity allows you to be compassionate with yourself.

Remember that achieving closure is not about passing or failing; it's about understanding your emotional landscape, making peace with your past, and ultimately finding a path forward that aligns with your well-being.

The Closure Test below comprises ten scenarios each followed by a set of three questions.

As you respond to each scenario and question, remember there are no right or wrong answers. Instead, the assessment aims to facilitate self-awareness and introspection.

Your emotional responses are valid and genuine, regardless of whether they align with societal expectations or norms.

In essence, this assessment recognizes that closure is a personal journey, and your unique perspective is the lens through which you evaluate your healing.

So, as you navigate through the scenarios, be open to discovering nuances about yourself, who you thought you were, and your healing journey so far.

Some of your responses may seem to contradict one another, but that is perfectly normal. This only confirms the complexity of your emotions and reveals the layers of issues you need to work on to achieve closure.

Your insights during the closure test will be immensely beneficial because you will be listening to a healing session concurrently. Your session will be more impactful, and you will experience deeper shifts and healing.

While this assessment aims to be a steppingstone towards closure, I acknowledge that revisiting certain memories and emotions can be triggering.

Please remember that you have the agency to engage with this test at your own pace.

If at any point you find that the questions are evoking overwhelming emotions, it's perfectly okay to set it aside and return to it when you feel more prepared, specifically after reading **STEP 2**.

Yes, you can jump to the next chapter only if you have attempted the Closure Test and found it too triggering.

Your emotional well-being is paramount, and you are under no obligation to complete this assessment if it feels too challenging now.

Your results will remain valid even if you read the entire book before coming back to it since you will still be able to subjectively assess your progress. You know how you are feeling!

The test simply offers a way to be consciously aware of those feelings and to measure your progress by the time you would have completed the steps outlined in this book.

I encourage you to approach the Closure Test with self-compassion and the understanding that healing is a gradual process.

By reflecting on these scenarios and questions in the Closure Test, you are taking a step towards gaining clarity, finding closure, and fostering a sense of renewal.

After each set of questions, take a moment to reflect and ask yourself two questions:

- "What am I feeling right now?"

- "What does this feeling mean to me?"

Strong emotions simply point you to the aspects and areas you need to work on to find closure.

So, name or label the feelings that come up. **Name up to 10 feelings, and rate them on a scale from 0 to 10, where 0 is "no pain" and 10 is "intense pain".**

If inclined, write your feelings and your thoughts in your journal. In fact, I strongly recommend you do so. Write freely, without censuring yourself.

This will serve as your honest baseline, your starting point, for the purposes of Closure Coaching through the rest of the book and beyond.

If you take the test, make sure you retake it after implementing the six steps outlined in this book, and you will be able to compare your results and assess your progress.

As mentioned earlier, I have prepared a Healing session for you, using my signature process called the **Somatic**

Resonance Method™ (I provide more details on this in **STEP 3**).

Make sure you play the healing session *WHILE* you are taking the Closure Test.

Because the scenarios and questions will trigger you, this healing session will act as a buffer and will help you contain, integrate, and transmute any negative feelings that come up, therefore preventing emotional flooding.

<u>Please, click here</u> to download the Healing Session or go to <u>https://rpb.li/AsalYB</u>

Once downloaded, it is time to press "PLAY" and get started with the Closure Test.

THE CLOSURE TEST™

Please, answer the following questions to the best of your ability and as honestly as possible.

Question 1: How long have you been on your journey to closure since your divorce, and do you feel that you have reached a point of acceptance and healing?

Question 2: If you could go back in time, would you have taken steps to expedite your healing process, or do you believe that the time you spent grieving was necessary for your personal growth and emotional well-being?

Question 3: Reflecting on the period of grief and emotional recovery since your separation or divorce, can you identify any specific costs or sacrifices you have made in terms of personal opportunities, career goals, or other life aspirations?

Question 4: Imagine an alternate scenario where you had been emotionally healthy and stable immediately after your divorce. In what ways do you believe your life journey would have been different, and what opportunities do you think you might have pursued?

Question 5: Are there specific opportunities, whether personal, professional, or social, that you feel you may have missed out on due to the emotional toll of your divorce and the subsequent healing process? Please share your thoughts on these missed opportunities and any lessons you've learned from them.

____

____

____

____

____

____

____

____

____

____

____

____

Question 6: Have you found any sources of comfort or support in your grief that you worry about letting go of as you work towards closure and emotional healing?

Question 7: What would you lose, if you found closure and moved on?

Question 8: Are there people in your life who stand to lose something if you found closure and moved on? What is their relationship with you and what exactly would they have to let go of?

Now, consider the following scenarios.

Scenario 1: After your divorce, you heard that your ex-spouse is in a new relationship and seems to be doing well.

Questions:

1. How do you generally feel about your ex-spouse's new relationship?

2. Do you find yourself comparing your own life to theirs? If so, how does it make you feel?

3. Does thinking about their new relationship still bring up any painful emotions for you?

- "What am I feeling right now?"

- "What does this feeling mean to me?"

	Name or label your feeling	Rate Your Feeling on a scale for 1 to 10
1		
2		
3		
4		
5		
6		
7		
8		
9		
10		

Any insights? Write your thoughts here.

When journaling or writing down your insights, avoid the following words: **"it"**, **"the"**, **"this"**, **"that"**.

Use **"I"**, **"my"**, **"me"**, and be specific, not evasive.

Scenario 2: Your ex-spouse achieves a personal or professional success that you had always hoped for during your marriage.

Questions:

1. How did you react when you learned about their success?

2. Have you found it challenging to be genuinely happy for them? Why or why not?

3. Does their success trigger any feelings of inadequacy or regret for you?

- "What am I feeling right now?"

- "What does this feeling mean to me?"

	Name or label your feeling	Rate Your Feeling on a scale for 1 to 10
1		
2		
3		
4		
5		
6		
7		
8		
9		
10		

Any insights? Write your thoughts here.

When journaling or writing down your insights, avoid the following words: **"it"**, **"the"**, **"this"**, **"that"**.

Use **"I"**, **"my"**, **"me"**, and be specific, not evasive.

Scenario 3: Your child speaks positively about spending time with your ex-spouse and their new partner.

Questions:

1. How do you feel when your child talks about their positive experiences with your ex-spouse's new partner?

2. Do you ever feel left out or replaced in your child's life? How do you cope with these emotions?

3. Does your child's relationship with your ex-spouse still bring up any emotional discomfort?

- "What am I feeling right now?"

- "What does this feeling mean to me?"

	Name or label your feeling	Rate Your Feeling on a scale for 1 to 10
1		
2		
3		
4		
5		
6		
7		
8		
9		
10		

Any insights? Write your thoughts here.

When journaling or writing down your insights, avoid the following words: **"it"**, **"the"**, **"this"**, **"that"**.

Use **"I"**, **"my"**, **"me"**, and be specific, not evasive.

Scenario 4: You unexpectedly run into your ex-spouse while they are on a romantic outing.

Questions:

1. How do you typically feel when you unexpectedly see your ex-spouse enjoying a romantic moment?

2. Does seeing them with someone else trigger any sense of longing or bitterness within you?

3. Do you avoid certain places or situations to prevent encountering your ex-spouse?

- "What am I feeling right now?"

- "What does this feeling mean to me?"

	Name or label your feeling	Rate Your Feeling on a scale for 1 to 10
1		
2		
3		
4		
5		
6		
7		
8		
9		
10		

Any insights? Write your thoughts here.

When journaling or writing down your insights, avoid the following words: **"it"**, **"the"**, **"this"**, **"that"**.

Use **"I"**, **"my"**, **"me"**, and be specific, not evasive.

Scenario 5: Your ex-spouse expresses remorse for their past actions that contributed to the divorce.

Questions:

1. How do you react when your ex-spouse acknowledges their mistakes from the past?

2. Are you able to accept their apology and move forward, or do you still harbor resentment?

3. Does thinking about their past behavior continue to evoke negative emotions?

- "What am I feeling right now?"

- "What does this feeling mean to me?"

	Name or label your feeling	Rate Your Feeling on a scale for 1 to 10
1		
2		
3		
4		
5		
6		
7		
8		
9		
10		

Any insights? Write your thoughts here.

When journaling or writing down your insights, avoid the following words: **"it"**, **"the"**, **"this"**, **"that"**.

Use **"I"**, **"my"**, **"me"**, and be specific, not evasive.

Scenario 6: A mutual friend shares news about your ex-spouse's life after the divorce.

Questions:

1. How do you generally feel when you receive updates about your ex-spouse from mutual friends?

2. Are you able to maintain healthy boundaries regarding the information you receive?

3. Does hearing about their life trigger any feelings of sadness or nostalgia?

- "What am I feeling right now?"

- "What does this feeling mean to me?"

	Name or label your feeling	Rate Your Feeling on a scale for 1 to 10
1		
2		
3		
4		
5		
6		
7		
8		
9		
10		

Any insights? Write your thoughts here.

When journaling or writing down your insights, avoid the following words: **"it"**, **"the"**, **"this"**, **"that"**.

Use **"I"**, **"my"**, **"me"**, and be specific, not evasive.

Scenario 7: Your ex-spouse begins dating someone who shares similar interests and hobbies with you.

Questions:

1. How do you react to the realization that they are dating someone with similar interests to yours?

2. Does this trigger any sense of competition or comparison? How do you manage these feelings?

3. Does their choice of partner still impact your emotional well-being?

- "What am I feeling right now?"

- "What does this feeling mean to me?"

	Name or label your feeling	Rate Your Feeling on a scale for 1 to 10
1		
2		
3		
4		
5		
6		
7		
8		
9		
10		

Any insights? Write your thoughts here.

When journaling or writing down your insights, avoid the following words: **"it"**, **"the"**, **"this"**, **"that"**.

Use **"I"**, **"my"**, **"me"**, and be specific, not evasive.

Scenario 8: You witness your ex-spouse enjoying a special occasion, such as a birthday or holiday.

Questions:

1. How do you feel when you see your ex-spouse celebrating special occasions without you?

2. Are you able to focus on your own happiness during similar occasions?

3. Does their enjoyment of these events still evoke any feelings of loss or resentment?

- "What am I feeling right now?"

- "What does this feeling mean to me?"

	Name or label your feeling	Rate Your Feeling on a scale for 1 to 10
1		
2		
3		
4		
5		
6		
7		
8		
9		
10		

Any insights? Write your thoughts here.

When journaling or writing down your insights, avoid the following words: **"it"**, **"the"**, **"this"**, **"that"**.

Use **"I"**, **"my"**, **"me"**, and be specific, not evasive.

Scenario 9: Your ex-spouse expresses interest in co-parenting more effectively for the sake of your child.

Questions:

1. How do you react to their willingness to work together for the benefit of your child?

2. Are you open to improving your co-parenting relationship, or do you still hold onto past grievances?

3. Does the idea of working with them trigger any feelings of mistrust or discomfort?

- "What am I feeling right now?"

- "What does this feeling mean to me?"

	Name or label your feeling	Rate Your Feeling on a scale for 1 to 10
1		
2		
3		
4		
5		
6		
7		
8		
9		
10		

Any insights? Write your thoughts here.

When journaling or writing down your insights, avoid the following words: **"it"**, **"the"**, **"this"**, **"that"**.

Use **"I"**, **"my"**, **"me"**, and be specific, not evasive.

____

____

____

____

____

____

____

____

____

____

____

Scenario 10: Your ex-spouse introduces their new partner to your child for the first time.

Questions:

1. How do you feel about your child meeting your ex-spouse's new partner?

2. Are you able to support your child's interactions with this new person, or does it bring up any negative emotions?

3. Does the thought of another person being close to your child still cause you distress?

- "What am I feeling right now?"

- "What does this feeling mean to me?"

	Name or label your feeling	Rate Your Feeling on a scale for 1 to 10
1		
2		
3		
4		
5		
6		
7		
8		
9		
10		

Any insights? Write your thoughts here.

When journaling or writing down your insights, avoid the following words: **"it"**, **"the"**, **"this"**, **"that"**.

Use **"I"**, **"my"**, **"me"**, and be specific, not evasive.

How are you feeling, overall, after the Closure Test? **Words to avoid when writing your insights: "it", "the", "this", "that". Use "I", "my", "me", and be specific, not evasive.**

Now, take a deep breath and let's dive into the six simple steps you will need to implement to find a healthy closure and set yourself up for a life of joy and purpose.

Step 1 - Play The Saturation Game

> *"You cannot solve a problem with the same mindset that created it."*
>
> -Albert Einstein

I already shared with you that I was four months pregnant when we separated. I fled what was my home for over ten years.

As you already know, divorce is a public thing. Something you cannot hide from your family or colleagues, as much as you would want things to be private.

Eventually, my colleagues heard about the split and supported me in various ways.

One colleague, I will never forget her, handed me two books. They were photocopies. She had read them and even made some notes in the margins.

She told me to take them home, read them, make my own copies if necessary. She promised they would change my life. I was surprised at the assertion and intrigued. But

I took them home, and that same night, I started reading the first one. I could not put it down.

I read it all night, and when I closed my eyes to sleep, I felt a new sense of purpose washing over me. The last chapter of the book is about non-resistance. When I closed the book, it felt like I embodied the spirit of non-resistance advocated by the author, Florence Scovel Shinn.

The book's title is "The Game Of Life and How To Play It". Yes, that's the same book I mentioned in the last chapter! (I can hear your exhale and relief from here – That's what closure, or taking your power back, feels like).

My entire focus shifted from "woe is me" and victimization to "bring it on"! I have read this book dozens of times since then. Every time I undertake a major project, I reread this book.

The second book was equally transformative: The Power Of Your Subconscious Mind by Joseph Murphy. These two books taught me about the power of affirmations, visualization, and imagination.

Most importantly, they taught me that everything I need is within me and made me realize the power of positive thinking and the Law of Assumption.

In my coaching, I make it a point to share these books with my clients, and I know from their feedback that these books open their eyes and minds to their potential, like nothing else.

We often hear the word "potential", but it is an abstract term for many people. It was for me, too. When I heard coaches say that, as human beings, we had unlimited potential, I struggled with the concept because of the limiting beliefs I held at the time and because this concept is quite challenging to define.

The analogy I found for the word "potential" is that it is like a full glass that never empties, no matter how much we pour from it. It is a reservoir of untapped capabilities and possibilities that lie within each one of us.

Imagine, if you will, a glass that never runs dry, constantly, and mysteriously replenishing itself. As we go through life, we can draw from this endless well of potential, like sips of inspiration and motivation.

Each sip fuels our journey, propelling us forward, and enabling us to accomplish our dreams and purpose.

These books enabled me to understand that I had potential and that it is truly limitless. I understood that I was always a choice away from changing the trajectory of my life, at every moment, and I did just that.

As a Closure Coach, I face the same challenge in getting my clients to realize that this potential exists within them too.

Many of us, myself included, often underestimate our own capacity for growth and transformation.

We allow self-doubt and fear to cloud our perception, convincing ourselves that our glass is half-empty instead of acknowledging the abundance within.

But once we come to understand the true nature of our potential, once we recognize that it is an ever-flowing stream that awaits our exploration, we can embrace a paradigm shift.

Only then can we begin to view ourselves not as stagnant vessels, but as dynamic beings with infinite possibilities at their feet.

Just like a glass that can be filled with different liquids, our potential too can take on various forms. It adapts and evolves as we do, allowing us to explore new skills, passions, and areas of expertise. It pushes us to expand our horizons and break free from the confines of our comfort zones.

The beauty of potential lies in its versatility. It is not confined to one path or one specific destination. It is a roadmap to self-discovery, providing us with endless avenues to explore and grow.

Like a glass that can hold water, wine, or even the mixture of the two, our potential enables us to embrace a myriad of experiences, encountering both success and so-called failure along the way.

When you understand the nature of your potential, you can actively tap into it and unlock it.

It only takes awareness to unlock your potential, this vast reservoir of capabilities that lies within you, and this first step of the Roadmap to Closure is the key to shifting your paradigm and expanding your awareness.

Play the saturation game!

So, the first step is to saturate your mind with thoughts, ideas and words that uplift and motivate you.

Anyone who has gone through a breakup or divorce knows what dark thoughts and negative emotions are.

Negative emotions rob us of our focus on things that empower us and direct our attention to things that weaken us.

They consume our thoughts, cloud our judgement, and hinder our progress. It is as if a thick fog envelops our mind, blurring our vision and inhibiting our ability to see the opportunities that surround us.

We must counter this negativity with positive thoughts and ideas. I know that when you grapple with hurt feelings, aligning your thoughts on something positive can be challenging.

However, I have found that using books both like a refuge and as a tool to divert your attention works tremendously well.

Read, even if you must read through tears.

Books have a magical way of transporting you to another world. They can inspire, uplift, and comfort you when you need it the most.

It is only through reading books like the ones I mentioned in the introduction that you will shift your mindset into a new gear that will propel you to the new chapter of your life.

I have curated a collection of 17 influential books that will provide you with the gentle nudge you need to reframe your perspective and embrace a brighter future. These are all the books in which I found companionship in my journey.

I believe that they possess a transformative power that can guide you through even the darkest of times.

They provide a sanctuary where you can anchor your dreams and find inspiration and the motivation to script the next chapter of your life.

These books will saturate your mind with a critical mass of new perspectives, fresh hopes, and profound wisdom that can help mend the soul's wounds and give you an unfair advantage over anyone who has yet to understand the true meaning of "potential".

These 17 books were my lifeline.

I know 17 books may seem a lot, but you can read all these in a month.

They do not require much of an investment either. Most of them are in the Public domain and are available on YouTube for free.

In the *Resources* section of this book, I will share a link where you can easily download all the audio files of the books I recommend, at least for those in the public domain.

If you truly want to move past your pain, find closure and thrive after divorce, you cannot afford to skip this step.

If you truly know what you want, then roll up your sleeves and get to work on yourself. These books will jolt you out of your comfort zone, elevate your mindset and your awareness, expand the realm of possibilities and opportunities for you. You are in for a treat!

These books became my coaches, and they helped me coach my children. I am a proud mom of six amazing children, inside and out.

As you immerse yourself in the pages of these thought-provoking books, prepared to be transformed.

Each author on this list holds a key to unlocking the vast potential within you, teaching you how to harness the power of your mind and reshape your destiny.

Here is the list of books and their authors, with a short description of how the ideas in their books can transform your life when you read with an open mind. I will even recommend you read them in this order if you have never read them.

The game of life and how to play it, by Florence Scovel Shinn.

This was the first book I read, and it shook me to my core. It helped me to believe in myself and Providence. My faith in God and in myself grew exponentially after reading this book. I understood that I had nothing to prove to anyone but to myself.

This book helped lay the foundation of my self-esteem and unwavering faith.

It is filled with powerful affirmations and compelling anecdotes to help you understand the laws of the universe.

You will discover how to align your thoughts and words with your deepest desires, manifesting a life filled with love, success, and fulfilment.

Listen On YouTube.
https://www.youtube.com/watch?v=9_52Za5k2Ck&t=9
5s

The Power of Your Subconscious Mind, by Joseph Murphy

This book will revolutionize your understanding of the mind's untapped potential. Murphy explores the depths of our subconscious and reveals how our thoughts shape our reality. This simple idea set off a cascade of lightbulbs in my mind!

The author shows how reprogramming your subconscious mind with positive affirmations can help you overcome limiting beliefs, attract abundance, and cultivate a happier and more fulfilling existence.

Listen On YouTube.

https://www.youtube.com/watch?v=iSNLoICPg0s

The Master key System, by Charles F. Haanel

The Master Key System outlines a comprehensive program for personal development and self-improvement. It is structured as a lesson series that guides you through mental focus, visualization, and positive thinking principles.

Haanel emphasizes the power of the subconscious mind and how it can be harnessed to achieve one's goals and desires. The book provides practical exercises to help you develop a greater sense of control over your thoughts, actions, and outcomes.

Listen on YouTube.

https://www.youtube.com/watch?v=kTnvPxyECS8

As A Man Thinketh, by James Allen

This concise work explores the connection between a person's thoughts and the outcomes they experience in life. The central idea is that people's thoughts shape their character and ultimately determine their circumstances.

Allen argues that cultivating positive and constructive thoughts can transform your life and achieve success and happiness.

The book emphasizes the power of self-control, mindfulness, and the importance of choosing one's thoughts deliberately. It will also help you to hold yourself accountable for your own missteps, which in many ways is liberating.

Listen on YouTube.

https://www.youtube.com/watch?v=iEq0dMu9vpk

Attaining your desires, Your invisible power and How to live life and Love It, Three books in one, by Genievieve Behrend

Genievieve Behrend reveals how belief can shape your reality, empowering you to manifest your dreams and live a life of purpose and abundance.

She provides practical exercises and guided meditations to take you on a transformative journey of self-discovery. She has a very compelling, down-to-earth style, just like Florence Scovel Shinn.

<u>Your Invisible Power.</u>

https://www.youtube.com/watch?v=jLNmdmIV7ys

<u>Attaining Your Desires.</u>

https://www.youtube.com/watch?v=k9pT1j28MjI&t=2888s

<u>How To Live Life And Love It.</u>

Open Your Mind to Receive, by Catherine Ponder

Catherine Ponder will guide you towards embracing the spiritual abundance the universe has in store for you.

Her teachings emphasize the importance of releasing negative beliefs and shifting your mindset towards abundance and prosperity.

By becoming open to receive, you will attract all you desire and realize that you deserve limitless blessings. This book reinforces your sense of worth and helps you to allow what's yours by divine right to come to you.

Listen On YouTube.

https://www.youtube.com/watch?v=JyyxD5VI_fg

The Secret, by Rhonda Byrne

Imagine a life where you can attract abundance, success, and happiness by simply changing your mindset.

The Secret took the world by storm when it was first released. It explores the concept of the Law of Attraction, which suggests that our thoughts and emotions profoundly influence the reality we experience. It explains the power of thoughts and beliefs in manifesting our desires.

It's not just about positive thinking; it's about embracing a mindset that aligns your thoughts, actions, and desires to create the life you truly want.

You'll gain insights into how your thoughts shape your reality and learn how to manifest your dreams and aspirations.

A movie was made out of this book, and it is freely available on YouTube.
https://www.youtube.com/watch?v=Ma_qMbvTpzo

Click here to watch.

The Magic of Thinking Big, by David J. Schwartz

In *The Magic of Thinking Big,* you are presented with a blueprint for success. Schwartz dismantles the limitations of a small mindset and challenges you to expand your horizons, redefine your goals, and overcome self-imposed barriers.

By changing your thoughts and adopting a positive mindset, you will discover the transformative power of thinking big, ultimately unlocking a world of opportunities.

Listen on YouTube.

https://www.youtube.com/watch?v=h0LCeM2LDCk

The Magic of Believing, by Claude Bristol

This is a masterpiece that explores the profound impact of our beliefs on our lives. Bristol encourages you to tap into your unlimited potential by harnessing the power of your mind.

Through engaging stories and strategies, he delves into the world of self-confidence, ambition, and the art of turning dreams into reality.

Prepare to be inspired and motivated to take bold steps towards achieving your desired life.

Listen on YouTube.

https://www.youtube.com/watch?v=t0H9gH11pQc&t=4431s

The Power of Positive Thinking, by Norman Vincent Peale

This is a timeless classic. It highlights the potential of positive thinking in overcoming challenges and achieving success. It teaches you how to reframe negative thoughts and situations, focus on optimism to ultimately improve your life.

Listen on YouTube.

https://www.youtube.com/watch?v=IjfPSiUn3eE&t=149s

The Alchemist, by Paulo Coelho

This book is Will Smith's favorite. It teaches us about following our dreams and the importance of listening to our hearts. It resonates with the notion that we can all discover our true calling.

Listen on YouTube

https://www.youtube.com/watch?v=8yY80KD14zg

The Four Agreements, by Don Miguel Ruiz

This is a spiritual guide to personal freedom.

This book shares four powerful agreements that, if practiced, can transform your life. It encourages us to be impeccable with our word, not to take anything personally, not to make negative assumptions, and always do our best.

Listen on YouTube.

https://www.youtube.com/watch?v=rWw20Q2KtzE

Busting Loose From The Money Game, by Robert Scheinfeld

This book takes you on a profound journey into your subconscious mind and challenges your beliefs about money and abundance.

It uncovers the hidden mechanisms influencing your financial reality and offers a practical guide to breaking free from this restrictive game.

Through proven techniques, it guides you in rewriting your financial blueprints.

It encourages you to let go of scarcity and embrace an abundant mindset, fostering a deep sense of worthiness and deservingness. It teaches how to align your thoughts, emotions, and actions with your desired outcomes to attract money and prosperity effortlessly. This is another one of my favorites. I reread it often.

Amazon Link.

https://www.amazon.ca/Busting-Loose-Money-Game-Mind-Blowing/dp/0470047496/

Think and Grow Rich, by Napoleon Hill

Think and Grow Rich is another timeless classic that unveils the secrets to success and wealth accumulation.

It emphasizes the power of positive thinking, persistence, and creating a burning desire to achieve your goals.

Listen on YouTube.

https://www.youtube.com/watch?v=ZUbfskQ-GAY&t=211s

The Power of Now, by Eckhart Tolle

This transformative book teaches us the importance of living in the present moment.

It guides us to let go of past regrets and future worries, allowing us to fully embrace the now and find inner peace.

Listen on YouTube.

https://www.youtube.com/watch?v=Zu_P1I9LQCc

Reality Transurfing Steps I to V, by Vadim Zeland

This unconventional and highly metaphysical book introduces the concept of "Reality Transurfing," which is a philosophy aimed at understanding and navigating the complexities of personal reality.

The book presents principles and techniques suggesting that reality is malleable and can be influenced by one's thoughts, intentions, and attitudes.

Zeland explains how to shift one's mindset, align intentions with goals, and detach from negative outcomes to create a more harmonious and successful life.

The steps outlined in the book offer a new perspective on your relationship with reality and how you can actively shape it.

Honestly, if you can buy and study one book, in this list, this is the one. The audio version is available on YouTube, but buying the book is worth it.

Listen On YouTube.

https://www.youtube.com/watch?v=K_A2S0a9a-k&list=PLJGapzWdofkn3dzkksSnZes7JVVpuKSsB

Sacred Contracts, by Caroline Myss

This book is not available on YouTube or for free. Look for it in your local library or buy it off Amazon or any bookstore. It is worth it.

Sacred Contracts is a spiritual self-help book where Myss introduces the concept of spiritual agreements and commitments that individuals make before birth.

She explores the idea that each person's life is guided by a pre-arranged set of archetypal patterns and lessons, which she refers to as sacred contracts.

Myss explores archetypes and how they impact our behavior, relationships, and life events. The book can provide you with insights into how archetypes contribute to our personal growth and journey of the soul.

Myss also explores the value of intuition and synchronicities in recognizing and completing these contracts.

Through self-exploration and reflection, she advises you to recognize your archetypal patterns and gain a more profound understanding of your life's purpose and direction.

Sacred Contracts combines spiritual teachings, psychological insights, and practical exercises.

Myss stresses the importance of aligning with your sacred contracts as it helps you live a more meaningful and fulfilling life that aligns with your higher purpose.

The book guides those seeking to understand the underlying spiritual forces that shape their existence and make choices aligned with their soul's purpose. I highly recommend it.

So, there you have it! These books and their authors are like lighthouses, calling you to navigate your way through the uncharted waters of your mind to explode your potential.

This is by no means an exhaustive list. Just an introductory one. In your downloads, you will find that I have added many other books, and I will continue to add more as I find them transformative.

Remember the words of Einstein, cited at the beginning of this chapter: ***"You cannot solve a problem with the same mindset that created it."***

This means that to reach higher levels, you must think and act from a higher plane of awareness.

As a single mom, you cannot afford to skip this step, you cannot afford to be lazy about working on your mindset. It is a question of survival.

It is a pre-condition for thriving in this life. I can even go as far as saying that there are valid reasons why you came on this path of divorce and divorce recovery, one of which being to sharpen your mindset and elevate your awareness.

These transformative books are a treasure trove of knowledge that will empower you to manifest your dreams and unlock your limitless potential.

Remember, the more you read and reread them, the more the teachings will be ingrained in your mind, driving your motivation, and propelling you to greatness. **In fact, I will challenge you here and now.**

Stop reading and click here to listen to _The Game Of Life And How To Play It_.

https://www.youtube.com/watch?v=Mu-es6rGfOE&t=237s

You can also search for it on YouTube. It will take you a little over two hours to listen to all of it.

Even if you have read it before, read it again with the intention of applying the insights towards your divorce recovery or healing journey.

Listen to the audiobook and watch what happens in the next few steps.

Step 2 - Clean The House

"Just let go"...

"Just move on"...

"Just forgive"...

"Time heals all wounds"...

"You'll be fine"...

"It gets better"...

"You are stronger than you think"...

"You are better off'...

Nothing frustrated me more than hearing such clichés and platitudes from people trying to comfort me. No one offered a true step-by-step process to heal my heart. No one showed me exactly what to do. They simply did not know.

You must have heard such clichéd statements yourself from well-meaning individuals attempting to console you as you navigate the tumultuous whirlwind of emotions brought on by your divorce or breakup.

I am also sure you have asked "how exactly does one move on?"

Over the past twenty years, I have asked myself hundreds of versions of this question.

Those questions stuck at the back of my mind and haunted me so much that the search for answers became my purpose.

For example, I would sit for my meditation on a specific subject, then my mind would wander to questions like:

Is there a way to neutralize those emotions in a healthy manner and quickly move on?

What's the most effective method for letting go and moving forward?

Are there strategies to deal with emotions and move on gracefully?

How can I find closure and transition to the next chapter of my life?

What are some practical steps for emotionally healing and moving forward?

Is there a formula for successfully putting the past behind and moving on?

What techniques can help me navigate through difficult emotions and move on smoothly?

Are there ways to speed up moving on while maintaining emotional well-being?

How can one detach from the past and embrace the future?

What's the secret to releasing emotional attachments and progressing in life?

Are there specific actions I can take to facilitate the process of moving on?

What strategies promote a healthy emotional recovery and the ability to move forward?

I stumbled upon the beginning of an answer five years ago.

As I investigated further, I tested it and created my signature process, the **Somatic Resonance method™**, which I have already used to help hundreds of women shorten their grieving period post-divorce, and step into their power.

I wish I had the **Somatic Resonance Method™** when I was going through pain, but I am glad I can make it available to single moms around the globe.

Armelle, one of my clients, recently sent me this message:

> *Your healing session on "Triggers-Objects" was a game changer. I held on to a lot of old objects from my marriage and every time I stumbled upon them, I would melt down. I would feel overwhelmed with emotions, and it was hard for me to move on from the past. But after just a few days of this session, I was able to let go of my*

wedding pictures, and my wedding dress, among other things. I don't get triggered by them anymore. Especially by my car. That is also one of the things I kept from my marriage, but I could not get into it without feeling a rush of very difficult emotions.

I am so grateful, because this healing session helped me to understand that my attachment to those objects were only holding me back. I am thankful that I was able to release the past and I now focus on the present. Now, when I see those things, I feel at peace, and I am grateful for the memories, but I am not trapped in them anymore. I highly recommend this session to anyone who is struggling with letting go of objects or memories from their past relationship.

Armelle, in a nutshell, summarized the goal and purpose of the **Somatic Resonance Method™**.

In **STEP 2**, you must do some deep house cleaning, physically and figuratively.

Your physical housecleaning entails cleaning up your environment, your room, your desk, your house, your car, etc.

This might seem like a ridiculous step to take, but it is vital for your mental wellbeing.

One other thing negative emotion robs us of is our sanity, which translates into neglect, a neglect of physical grooming needs, a neglect of our kids and our homes, etc., although in rare cases, it can also translate into extreme OCD.

So many single moms suffer from undiagnosed depression and neglect is usually one of the most obvious signs.

As within, so without.

Your surroundings reflect your mindset.

There is another not so obvious reason why it is necessary to take action physically in such a way.

Your activity is a way to anchor your intention to heal in your environment. You are dusting off your path to healing externally and internally.

You are engaging your neurology and clearly yet subtly communicating to your parts that this is your new intention, and you need them to be in alignment with this intention, you need them to be on your team.

You are also signaling to the universe that you are ready to jump into a new lifeline, a new experience of life, and you are entering into a new dimension of opportunities and possibilities.

You will even feel it while you are at it. You will feel energized and, for those who are sensitive enough, you will sense your heart or your solar plexus warming up.

This is just the echo of the universe's "YES!" to your new intentions and your new choices.

So, it is an auspicious time to milk this feeling and give it amplitude, to activate what Vadim Zeland, the author of Reality Transurfing, calls the wave of fortune.

Housecleaning, figuratively this time, entails decluttering your mind, your energy systems, your meridians, your heart, of all the emotions, memories, behaviors, beliefs, attitudes that have been keeping you hostage to your past.

Healing sessions are my favorite approaches to achieve this, and don't worry, I will show you how to have easy access to them.

Healing sessions based on my SRM™ offer a safe, non-judgmental space to explore your thoughts, emotions, and experiences and transmute them instantly.

These sessions also allow you to gain insights into your feelings, your behaviors, and your patterns, heal past wounds, and develop healthier coping mechanisms.

When used as instructed, they can be life-changing and offer a sanctuary where you can delve into your inner self, heal your wounds, and ultimately create a more fulfilling and empowered life.

My signature process, **The Somatic Resonance Method® (SRM™)** is a synthesis of my learning about many healing modalities proven to be very effective in resolving emotional issues on their own, which I have married with my understanding of human neurology and the efficacy of the spiritual notion of "standing in the gap". The result is a potent and transformative healing process.

I have been trained and Certified and I am a facilitator of these modalities, including MAP™ (Making Anything Possible), Emotional Freedom Technique (EFT) and Thought Field Therapy (TFT), Neurolinguistic Programming (NLP), Cognitive Behavioral Therapy (CBT) and Sacred Body Language Translations (SBLT).

The main principle underpinning these healing sessions is that our nervous system can be primed in various ways to echo our intentions, positive or negative, and activated to create or resolve issues quietly.

In other words, your nervous system was influenced to create the emotional issues you are facing today as they relate to your divorce or breakup, because your entire neurology was also engaged in that relationship in a more active way than you think.

This led to the creation of a multitude of anchor points, like nodes, in your system. You need to influence your neurology now to loosen those nodes, to release their grip, and set you free.

The pain you are feeling after divorce or breakup is because normally, those anchor points, those nodes, need to be nurtured and fed through the relationship.

However, because of the breakup or divorce, they are starved, and your pain is feedback from them.

You will not be at peace until either you throw them a bone, by compensating through another relationship, there's a reason it is called a rebound, or you find a healthy closure process like the one I outlined in this book.

The healing sessions therefore act as your internal soap or shampoo; it will lubricate the nodes and anchors in your system and make it easier to unravel them and bring you closure.

Most people see results within the first few hours of exposure to audio healing sessions made with the **Somatic Resonance Method**®.

The Somatic Resonance Method® has already helped hundreds, if not thousands, of women who approached me with feelings of hopelessness and despair after their breakups.

Within days, they were no longer focused on their pain. They started talking about their projects with a renewed sense of purpose.

At the end of this chapter, I will share with you how to avail yourself of my collection of impactful and fast-acting audio healing sessions based on **The Somatic Resonance Method®**, specifically designed to help people, and especially single moms, move on faster, find closure and thrive.

With **The Somatic Resonance Method®** you can put the past behind you and focus on your future with a clean slate.

This internal cleaning is crucial to make space for personal growth and allow positive energy to flow into your life. It is a journey that requires self-reflection, honesty, and the willingness to confront any lingering baggage from your past.

In these healing sessions, I will guide you through various techniques to help you release and let go of these negative emotions that have been holding you back.

Each session is carefully designed to target specific issues. As you engage in these healing sessions, you will begin to feel the weight of resentment, for example, lift from your shoulders. The burdens of jealousy and anger will gradually dissipate as you nurture a sense of compassion and forgiveness for yourself and for others.

These sessions will empower you to confront your fears head-on and embrace a life free from the limitations of past traumas.

As you explore the depths of your consciousness, you will uncover the root causes of some of your fears, issues, and patterns, shining a compassionate light on the dark corners that hold you back.

Through these transformative sessions, you will peel away the layers of past traumas, gently unraveling their hold on your mind, your spirit, and your life.

Embracing a life free from the limitations of past traumas requires courage, vulnerability, and a deep willingness to face the uncomfortable. That is how you take your power back, not by shunning or bottling up your feelings and your fears.

In the safety of this healing space provided by the healing session, you will learn to reframe your past traumas as steppingstones toward growth and resilience.

This will help you to neuter the painful memories and transmute them into valuable lessons, allowing you to break free from the shackles of the past and shape a future filled with possibilities.

You will nurture your inner resilience, fostering a mindset that enables you to face adversity with unwavering strength.

You will notice profound shifts occurring within you.

You will replace the limiting beliefs with the empowering beliefs that you are worthy, deserving, and capable of creating a life filled with joy, fulfillment, and unlimited potential.

You will witness the gradual shedding of old beliefs and negative thought patterns, allowing new, empowering narratives to emerge. You will build a solid foundation for your emotional well-being.

Remember that this is not a linear journey. There may be moments of discomfort, resistance, and even setbacks.

But know that these are all part of your growth process, and I and the community will be here to support you through each turn.

You hold the keys to your own freedom and liberation. The power to heal, grow, and create a life free from the shackles of the past lies within you.

If you have succeeded at anything before, which I know you have, you can succeed in this too.

You are wired to overcome. The wiring is there. You only need to plug it in, using the healings sessions.

Remember the Closure Test, it will prove invaluable here as well.

I recommend you evaluate your progress often. As you progress, you will find that the past no longer holds power over your present, and your focus will naturally shift toward the possibilities of the future.

You will unveil your own brilliance.

I have created a collection of over 50 healing sessions specifically targeting various emotional states and issues associated with divorce or separation.

For example, jealousy is one of the most debilitating feelings we can experience after divorce when we see our ex-partner move on.

This can trigger feelings of worthlessness and anger because we feel used and disposable.

The audio healing session addresses the different layers of this issue completely and with compassion.

It is fast and effective.

When you take the Closure Test AFTER a Somatic Resonance Session, you will be able to tell the difference almost immediately.

Audio healing sessions based on the Somatic Resonance Method and instructions are available for instant download on my website at

STEP 2 is one of the most crucial steps in this process if you want to fast-track your healing and closure.

Step 3 - On Your Marks!

On your marks, get set, go!

I want to share a thought that struck me recently, inspired by the simple yet powerful phrase, "On your marks, get set, go!"

It's amazing how this phrase, often associated with races and competitions, can mirror our journey through life and our pursuit of success.

Much like a plane before takeoff or a car before hitting the road, humans need a moment to prepare before launching into their endeavors.

Just as engines need to be warmed up to perform at their best, we, too, need to find ways of getting into the optimal mindset before embarking on our tasks.

Imagine standing at the start line of a race, feeling the anticipation and excitement building within you. This moment is not just about physical readiness but also about our mental and emotional preparedness.

It's a chance to gather our thoughts, set our intentions, and harness the energy needed to give our best shot at whatever lies ahead.

Life is full of challenges and opportunities that require us to be prepared mentally, emotionally, and sometimes even spiritually.

Just like the engine's warmth ensures a smoother takeoff, our preparedness equips us to tackle obstacles with resilience and embrace opportunities enthusiastically.

So, as you navigate the various layers of your recovery and healing post-divorce, take moments to pause, reflect, and get ready to allow yourself to step into your endeavors with purpose and determination.

The process of getting ready is as significant as the result. Embrace moments of stillness before action and use them to align your thoughts and intentions.

In STEP 3, I will strongly emphasize self-care, prayer for believers, and meditation or simply silence.

Find time for yourself. To get on your marks.

First, allocate time daily to sit still. There is no such thing as "doing nothing".

You are always doing something, and even your stillness is an activity, as it powerfully influences the spiritual realm.

Actually, sitting still, even for 5 minutes a day can be the hardest thing to do for some people, because they are afraid to confront their thoughts and their minds.

If this is the case for you, get any healing session (even the one provided along with this book will perfectly do), play it and sit still and passively for as long as you can.

Sit still with the intention to reconnect with yourself in a deeper way, to allow yourself to feel what it feels like to be healed.

I call these interludes "snaps", because they snap you out of your hypnotic routine and force you to be awake and aware.

Practicing snaps is a very powerful way to usher out the hold of your negative patterns and they are also ideal moments to practice visualization and constitute great preparation to practice some other advanced future programming techniques like the Plait technique, which is out of the scope of this book.

After your snaps, engage in activities that rejuvenate your mind, body, and soul. Explore hobbies that bring you joy and fulfilment, whether painting, dancing, walking, or exploring nature.

Regular exercise improves your physical health and releases endorphins that can boost your mood and overall sense of well-being.

Combining self-care, prayer, and meditation can lead you on a path of transformation, helping you find inner peace and spiritual growth.

It is essential to carve out dedicated time for yourself amidst the hustle and bustle of daily life. For single moms, this is vital.

I wish I understood this sooner. I did not, and one day, I was rushed to the hospital, only to be diagnosed with high blood pressure.

Remember, self-care is not a luxury. With your self-care, you buy more time to be with your children and grandchildren.

Self-care has to do both with your outer appearance and your inner state, and the tools are prayer, meditation and silence, exercise, self-grooming.

At times, I've encountered clients who have raised objections regarding the sequence of steps outlined in this book, particularly asserting that Prayer should take precedence.

However, my response to this matter remains resolute and unwavering: a firm and unequivocal NO!

Allow me to reiterate the profound words of Albert Einstein: "You cannot resolve a problem with the same mindset that created it."

This quote encapsulates a fundamental truth that must not be overlooked.

The notion that Prayer should be the initial step contradicts the very essence of transformative change.

If one were to delve into prayer with their existing frame of mind or mindset, the outcome is likely to be a repetition of the familiar patterns and outcomes.

This is akin to attempting to mend a broken vessel using the same flawed materials that led to its fracture. That's the definition of insanity. Doing the same things over and over, expecting different results.

Instead, I stand by the approach I have advocated so far. Engaging with transformative self-help literature serves as a catalyst for evolution. These texts act as a beacon, guiding you toward introspection and growth.

They challenge preconceived notions, broaden perspectives, and introduce new paradigms. By immersing yourself in these texts, a metamorphosis occurs – a shift in perception that lays the groundwork for meaningful change.

Contrary to the notion of prayer being the first step, this approach complements Einstein's wisdom. By altering one's mindset through the absorption of transformative literature, you cultivate a new mental landscape from which to approach your prayers.

This shift is crucial, empowering prayers with renewed vigor and effectiveness. It's comparable to equipping oneself with the appropriate tools before undertaking a challenging endeavor.

The sequence of steps advocated here harmonizes with the very nature of change – a departure from the familiar and a journey toward new horizons. Einstein's words remain an indelible reminder that change requires a departure from the status quo.

So, I will encourage you to embrace the catalyst nature of these transformative self-help books before delving into prayer. This sets the stage for authentic, impactful change.

Suspend your judgment and pick up just one book, *The Game Of Life And How To Play It*, if you have not yet done so.

You will immediately notice a change in the substance of your prayer. I hope you took the time to read and listen to the audio from the link provided in the previous chapter.

If you did, I bet your prayers no longer sound as shallow, and you pray with more conviction and assurance.

This paradigm shift truly enhances the potency of your prayers, enabling you to transcend limitations and approach challenges with newfound strength and insights.

When you elevate your mindset by reading the books in **STEP 1**, you upgrade yourself, and now you pray for a place of certainty, of victory. You pray confidently, and your dreams are more likely to manifest quickly.

With the books you have read from **STEP 1** you will gradually cultivate a heightened sense of awareness, bringing a sense of calm and tranquility into your life.

Again, it is crucial to recognize that prayers and meditations are most effective when approached with the right mindset.

If your heart is burdened by defeat, anger, resentment, or any other negative emotions, take the time to work through them before or while engaging in these practices. Address the root causes of these emotions with the tools provided to you in **STEP 2**.

Exercise and self-grooming are also two vital components of self-care that can significantly impact your mental and emotional well-being.

While the challenges of single parenthood can be overwhelming, neglecting one's physical and grooming needs can lead to a negative spiral.

Here's why exercise and self-grooming are essential for your holistic health:

1. **Boosted Confidence:** Regular exercise and self-grooming practices can contribute to an enhanced sense of self-confidence.

When you take time to care for your physical well-being, you start to feel better about yourself. The endorphins released during exercise can uplift your mood while self-grooming rituals provide a sense of accomplishment and self-worth.

Divorce is extremely damaging to women's sense of worth and self-esteem, and self-grooming might seem superficial, but it is a core element of a woman's mental stability.

Examples of self-grooming practices are:

- **Skincare Routine:** Establishing a skincare routine can have a significant impact on one's appearance and self-confidence. This might involve cleansing, exfoliating, applying moisturizer, and using sunscreen to protect the skin. Taking care of the skin can boost self-esteem and provide a sense of rejuvenation.

- **Hair Care:** Maintaining healthy hair can greatly contribute to a polished appearance. This includes regular washing, conditioning, and styling. You can consider hair treatments, trims, and experimenting with different hairstyles to express yourself and boost your self-esteem. I have seen women shave their hair or change their hairstyle post6divorcem and this helped to boost their self6estee.

- **Nail Care:** Keeping nails clean and well-groomed can make a noticeable difference in your appearance. This simple ritual can add a touch of elegance to your overall look.

- **Makeup Application:** Applying makeup, if desired, can be an enjoyable self-grooming activity. Even a minimal makeup routine can help enhance facial features and boost self-confidence. You can explore makeup tutorials and techniques that align with your personal style.

- **Relaxing Baths:** A relaxing bath can be a calming self-care ritual. Adding scented oils, bath salts, or bubbles to the water can create a soothing atmosphere, promoting relaxation and emotional well-being.

- **Scented Rituals:** Using scented products such as perfumes, body lotions, or essential oils can positively impact your mood. These fragrances can evoke pleasant memories and sensations, contributing to a sense of comfort and relaxation (if some scents and perfumes evoke painful memories, visit the website for a healing session on this aspect).

- **Dressing Up:** Putting effort into selecting and coordinating outfits can boost your self-esteem and confidence. You can experiment with your wardrobe, mixing and matching clothing items to create stylish and comfortable ensembles that reflect your personality.

- **Facial Care:** Treating yourself to a facial at home or through a spa can rejuvenate your skin and provide a refreshing feeling. This ritual can help you feel pampered and cared for.

- **Body Care:** Regularly moisturizing your body, using body scrubs, and dry brushing can promote healthy skin and a sense of physical well-being.

- **Groomed Eyebrows:** Keeping eyebrows well-groomed can frame the face and enhance facial symmetry. This simple ritual can make a noticeable difference in your overall appearance.

You get the idea. Find something that you like to do to pamper yourself. A trip to the spa, or to the nail salon, that's what I like to treat myself to.

Remember, self-grooming rituals are about taking time for oneself, enhancing self-esteem, and promoting self-care.

You can choose the rituals that resonate with you and tailor them to fit your lifestyle and preferences.

These practices not only contribute to a polished appearance but also nurture a positive mindset and emotional balance.

1. **Stress Relief:** Juggling the responsibilities of single parenthood can be incredibly stressful. Physical activity, such as jogging, yoga, or dancing, releases tension and reduces stress hormones. This, in turn, promotes mental clarity and emotional balance, helping single mothers tackle their challenges with a clearer mind.

2. **Positive Body Image:** Regular exercise helps maintain a healthy body weight and shape, contributing to a more positive body image. By feeling stronger and healthier, you can combat negative self-perceptions and develop a healthier relationship with your body. Self-grooming adds to this positivity by allowing you to present yourself in a way that reflects your inner vitality.

3. **Time for Self:** Incorporating exercise and self-grooming into your routine provides you with dedicated "me-time." This time allows you to momentarily disconnect from your parenting responsibilities and focus on self-care. It's a chance

to recharge and rejuvenate, which can profoundly impact your overall emotional well-being and your children's.

4. **Sense of Normalcy:** Amid the seeming chaos of single parenting, exercise and self-grooming routines can provide a sense of normalcy. Following a routine, even in small ways, can create a structure that brings stability and a sense of control to your life.

5. **Social Interaction:** Participating in group exercise classes or outdoor activities can facilitate social interaction, combatting feelings of isolation that most single mothers' experience. Connecting with others who share similar interests can foster a supportive community and reduce feelings of loneliness and stress.

6. **Emotional Release:** Physical activity offers a healthy outlet for emotional release. Exercise provides a safe space to channel and process emotions, leading to emotional relief and clarity.

In essence, exercise and self-grooming are not just about outward appearances; they are crucial in cultivating a positive mental and emotional state.

Prioritizing self-care enhances your overall well-being, empowers you to tackle the demands of single parenthood with resilience, confidence, and a greater sense of balance.

When you dedicate time to your physical and grooming needs, you acknowledge your own worth, setting the stage for a more fulfilled and emotionally resilient life.

Commit yourself to prioritizing these practices, continuously refining them as you evolve and grow.

Step 4 - Write Your Gospel

"Write it. Believe it. Achieve it."

- Germany Kent

This new chapter of your life will unfold according to your Gospel.

I have learned that life is an unfoldment, a deployment of my thoughts, my imagination, my desires, and my dreams.

You create your own reality, whether you believe it. Your life today is the reflection of your past thoughts and actions. This is a powerful notion to be aware of, and a potent source of power because this means that you have a certain level of control, of responsibility and of authority over your life experience.

Avery thought you entertain, every decision you make and every action you take has the potential to shape your future. It is through your thoughts, imagination, desires, and dreams that you can manifest your own reality.

Harnessing the power within yourself is all about being a witness to yourself. It is all about being your observer and being more intentional.

Now is the time to sow seeds and plant the thoughts according to the fruits you desire to harvest, and not by default.

What do you truly desire in life? What does a successful life look like to you? What would make this life worthwhile to you?

Take a moment to ponder these questions. Within your answer also lies the essence of your purpose.

Your desires, dreams, and aspirations define the path you tread upon, guiding your every decision and shaping your destiny.

Writing your own gospel will enable you to have a solid framework upon which to anchor your thoughts, your dreams, and aspirations. It is what you will fall back on, draw your inspiration from, and stand on to move further and thrive.

Your gospel helps you not only filter your thoughts, but it also helps filters your relationships, your choices, your priorities and even your expenditure.

It helps you to magnetize experiences, things, people, thoughts, and patterns that are in sync with who you are becoming, while putting a distance between you and everything else that does not match your current vibes.

Your Gospel is your compass. It is a buffer around you and a guard around your thoughts.

Making your gospel entails three steps:

- Clarify your values

- Create your amalgamation statement

- Scripture your path ahead.

Clarify Your Values

A new day has come.

What are the things, attitudes, and patterns that you will no longer tolerate from yourself or from others around you?

I decided not to tolerate any disrespect and any apathy, on my part and from people around me. I set my boundaries and, since it was clear in my mind that I would not accept anything short of respect, I was at peace. This freed up my energy, reduced my stress levels, and enabled me to create more space for positive experiences and relationships with my children.

What are your priorities and your non-negotiables?

What are the positive traits or behaviors that you admire in others and would like to cultivate in yourself?

Who or what can hold you accountable for living according to your new values, and how will you engage this accountability

Once you are clear on your values, it will be like drawing a bold line between the old you and the new you.

Write a statement about your new set of values, starting with: "A new day has come, and I, _______________".

Here is an example: *A new day has come, and I, Mary, have decided to no longer tolerate negativity in my life. My children and I are my top priorities, and I will not allow anything or anyone to compromise our well-being. We are the most important thing to each other. No one can treat us badly or be unkind to us. I will not allow it. I will not accept disrespect or unkindness from others, and I will not let self-doubt or past failures define my future success. My dreams are just as worthy, and I am committed to pursuing them with all the positivity and perseverance I can muster. This is my pledge for a brighter, more fulfilling future for myself and my children.*

Most people only know what they want after they have clarified what they do not want anymore, and this first step allows you to clarify where you stand emotionally and mentally.

The energy you will project after clarifying your values will be a statement people will understand just for your presence, without you even saying a word. This is how you teach people how to treat you.

Now is your turn. Write a statement that encapsulates your new set of values:

A new day has come, and I,

____

____

Create your amalgamation statement

I remember the exact day I found mine and settled with it.

It had been a particularly rough week, and I was short on funds. Then, my cousin passed away. It was in early June. I was pregnant and due in two weeks. I had no savings or money to register my children in school for September.

I was on the roadside, waiting for a taxi to take me to my aunt's house, where the family gathered to prepare the funerals and the weight of everything just hit me like a ton of bricks, and I started weeping.

I did my best to hide it, but tears kept coming. Then, without any care in the world, I started talking to God aloud.

I said, "You gave me these children. You had better take care of them. You better provide for them. I am not asking anything for myself. I don't know what to do anymore! From today, I will not worry about a single thing. I give up worrying. You take care of this stuff because I can't. You can't possibly give me kids and not give me the means to take care of them! What wrong have I done? I have been doing my best here, I have been trying, I am trying, but now, you take over!! "

I kept on rambling like that and only stopped when a taxi pulled up in front of me.

As I dried my tears, mainly because I did not want to appear crazy to the other people in the taxi, a phrase came to mind *"God will provide, God provides, God is my Source"*.

This statement spoke to me like never before, and I kept repeating it internally.

My prayers only consisted of these words from then on. I repeated them hundreds of times per day! This became my mantra; my amalgamation statement.

An amalgamation statement is a phrase that resonates deeply with you and embodies your outlook and philosophy of life. Something you know is true, or you want to be true.

While reading Reality Transurfing, I later understood why this is so powerful. Your Amalgamation statement underpins your intention for your life experience in this reality. It sets the compass of your reticular activating system firmly on the trajectory of this intention. More about this in the next step.

Sometimes I have amended my Amalgamation statement to *"everything works out for me"* or *"this too shall pass"* or, *"my world takes care of me"*, but *"God is my Source"* has always been my favorite.

What is your amalgamation statement?

If you do not have any, it is time to create one and saturate your subconscious mind with it. Write it on sticky notes, screensaver, or palm of your hand if you need to.

Stick it to your mirror, fridge, and doors everywhere you can until you can feel the truth of it. Then watch what happens!

Doors will open, creative ideas will flood your mind, and you will experience an avalanche of synchronicities and opportunities. I recommend you keep your journal or a notebook handy.

Create your amalgamation statement:

____

____

____

____

____

____

____

____

Scripture your life

The last step in writing your own Gospel is to Scripture your life.

What are some specific goals you can set that reflect your new values, and what is your plan to achieve them?

At the beginning of every year, I list 100 things I would like to accomplish in the next 12 months.

Sometimes, I even go beyond the year to write my dreams and aspirations for the next two, five or ten years. I cannot begin to tell you how magical this exercise is.

Sometimes, I return to my list a few months later, only to realize I can cross some items off because they already came true.

Clarify what your desires, dreams, and aspirations are. Clarify your needs and keep a journal where you scripture your dreams.

It is imperative to clarify your desires, to define them with crystalline clarity, to harness the power within you to bring them to fruition.

Your desires, aspirations, and intentions are the compass that directs your energy and fuels your motivation to push beyond any obstacles.

In the pursuit of your desires, it is essential to acknowledge your needs: emotional, intellectual, physical, and spiritual. Take the time to identify and understand what nourishes your soul and ignites that fervent flame within you.

Next, to ensure that your desires remain at the forefront of your being.

Your journal is more than just a collection of pages and words; it is a place where you anchor your aspirations to the physical realm through the written word, therefore lending them substance and strength.

Scribbling your dreams onto paper is the first step to their embodiment and empowers you to take the necessary steps towards their physical realization.

Human beings are the only species God gave the power to write to. Your writing is scripture for your life.

As the only species bestowed with the gift of writing, we hold tremendous power within our hands – the power to create, inspire, and illuminate our own paths. Words, etched onto the pages of your journal, become your scripture.

They will not become true. They are true.

If you have read any of the books listed in STEP 1, you already have an insight into the truth of this statement. If you need more convincing, do the exercise below and judge for yourself.

Take the time to scripture 100 or 200 dreams you have, the things you would like to accomplish in the next six months, two years, five years, ten years!

Don't limit yourself. Your imagination is said to be God's laboratory. Use it to the fullest. You are only limited by the limits of your imagination in this exercise. All you need is literally within you now.

Your dream home, your dream car, your dream business, etc., are already within you. If you see it clearly in your mind, you already have it. Writing about it firmly anchors it in this physical realm and starts to give it substance. This is the substance everything in this physical realm is made up of.

You are denying yourself if you limit your imagination. In the parable of the Prodigal son, don't be the son who stayed home and could not even enjoy the riches before him.

In the realm of limitless possibilities, your imagination is a divine gift that allows you to explore your creative potential's depths. It is the gateway to a world where dreams are true.

When you fully embrace the power of your imagination, you become a master of your own destiny.

The ideas and concepts that take shape within your mind become the seeds of greatness, waiting to be nurtured and brought forth into reality.

Let your imagination run wild. Allow it to wander through the vast landscapes of your thoughts, unbridled and untamed.

In the laboratory of your mind, experiment with different scenarios, characters and versions of yourself and worlds.

Scripturing anchors your desires in this physical reality. Your sustained focus and emotional alignment, and detachment accelerate their manifestation.

If you find it difficult to be emotionally aligned and detached, meaning you notice you are fretting or needy, the next **STEP 5** will be even more helpful and cathartic for you.

Remember that your imagination knows no limits except those you impose on it yourself.

It is the key that unlocks the door to infinite possibilities. So, dare to dream, dare to imagine, and dare to create.

Have you read *The Magic Of Thinking Big Yet?*

Remember that desires, dreams, and aspirations are not meant to be stagnant.

They are ever evolving, adapting to the rhythms of your life and the world around you.

Be gentle with yourself, celebrate your big and small victories, and forgive yourself for the occasional missteps.

Remember, your dreams define your reality. What you see in your imagination is not a mere illusion, but a manifestation waiting to unfold.

As you scripture these dreams onto the canvas of your life, take practical steps toward their realization, with the child-like assurance that you will be guided.

This list of dreams is your dream board. Break them into actionable goals, draw up a roadmap, and consistently take action.

Believe in your ability to transform the words on your dream board into tangible achievements.

Do not let fear or doubt cloud your vision. If you can visualize it, you can achieve it.

Scripture a future worth living, a life driven by purpose, and a legacy that will endure.

Embrace the wondrous ability God bestowed upon you – the power to write the story of your own extraordinary life.

Again, when writing your list, do not place any limitations on yourself or on the power that created you.

Do not worry about HOW your dreams will unfold because the power that created you has ways you know nothing about.

Instead, trust in the infinite wisdom and boundless potential of the universe. Allow yourself to dream big and imagine a life filled with limitless possibilities.

See yourself becoming a source of inspiration, radiating positivity, and touching the lives of others with your words and actions. See the greatest good of all who cross paths with you in this dream life.

Picture yourself pursuing your passions, whether as an acclaimed artist, a renowned scientist, a celebrated entrepreneur, or a compassionate healer, a teacher, a nurse, a writer, etc.

Imagine honing your skills and talents, pushing the boundaries of what is known, and making groundbreaking discoveries that benefit mankind.

Visualize a life filled with abundance, where financial prosperity flows effortlessly, enabling you to enjoy all the luxuries and experiences you desire.

Picture yourself surrounded by loved ones, creating cherished memories, and basking in the joy of deep connections.

Imagine a world where you are in perfect harmony with your body, mind, and spirit. See yourself radiating vibrant health and vitality, effortlessly maintaining balance and well-being.

Picture yourself engaging in activities that nourish your soul, bringing you inner peace and contentment.

As you write your list, remember that the universe does not distinguish between big and small dreams. It hears the desires of your heart, no matter how grandiose or humble they may seem.

Trust that the power that created you knows the perfect path to bring your dreams to fruition.

Release any worries about the HOW, as it is not your responsibility to figure out the intricate details of the journey. Instead, focus on aligning yourself with the energy of your dreams, taking inspired action, and surrendering to the divine timing of their manifestation.

Believe with unwavering faith that your dreams are within reach. Embrace a mindset of limitless possibilities and let go of any self-imposed limitations. Embrace the unknown as you write your list and pour your heart and soul into it.

If you find it challenging to adopt a mindset of limitless possibilities, I will recommend your read the book *Reality*

Transurfing I recommended in STEP 1. The concept of possibilities will effortlessly seep into your consciousness.

Revisit your list occasionally, preferably at night before going to bed. This works.

Taking a few moments to review your list awakens a powerful force within you - your reticular activating system.

The reticular activating system, or RAS, is an intricate network of nerve fibers that connects the brainstem to the cerebral cortex. It is responsible for filtering and processing information from our environment, both externally and internally.

Revisiting your list signals to your RAS that these goals and dreams crystallize your intention. The RAS then directs your attention toward opportunities, experiences, and resources that align with your desires.

Think of it as a map for your subconscious mind. Your RAS identifies the coordinates, and your subconscious acts as the compass, guiding you toward the path that will lead to your desired destination.

Visualizing your dreams before sleep helps set the stage for your subconscious to work its magic throughout the night when you are the most able to let go and your critical factors are out of the way.

As you lie down to rest, your mind begins to drift into a state of relaxation. It becomes more susceptible to suggestion and impression. This is when the true power of revisiting your list comes into play.

Imagine yourself already living the life you envision. See yourself succeeding, thriving, and achieving those goals that you hold closest to your heart.

The power of visualization and revisiting your list before sleep cannot be overstated.

In your dreams, your aspirations and desires intertwine with the magic of your imagination, allowing you to explore possibilities that may seem far-fetched in your waking hours.

Activating your reticular activating system before bed is not merely a bedtime routine. It is a sacred ritual connecting you to the infinite potential within you.

So, as you lay your head upon your pillow at night, take a moment to revisit your dream board.

Give your reticular activating system something to work with and. As Bob Proctor said, If you can see it in your mind, you can hold it in your hands.

What are your dreams, desires, and aspirations? Take a moment now to write anything that comes to mind, without filtering or analyzing.

Step 5 - Touch The Sun

During one-on-one sessions with my clients, in-person or over Zoom, I am always eager to get to the part of **The Somatic Resonance Method®** where I help them let the sun in their hearts.

Without fail, every single time, I get to witness the moment where the word "gratitude" is embodied and no longer feels like a vain word to them.

They experience gratitude in a profound and cathartic way.

For the first time, they feel grateful to tears, and every inch of their body feels inhabited by the same feeling of peace, gratitude, and elation.

Gratitude is powerful.

Be grateful for what you already have to open doors for more. Be grateful for who you are and who you are becoming. Be grateful for everything you are aware of, and for the blessings you are not aware of.

You can even take your gratitude exercise a step further.

Grab a journal and write what you are grateful for every day. You already know the power of your writing.

In the pages of your journal, let the ink flow and illuminate the countless reasons for which you are grateful.

Write fervently, imbuing each word with the remembrance of the blessings you received and of those on the way.

There is certainly something in your life you can bring yourself to be grateful for.

Start with the simplest things, the ones often taken for granted – the tender warmth of the morning sun caressing your face, the symphony of birds serenading the dawn, the cool breeze.

With each passing day, embrace the opportunity to express gratitude for the tangible aspects of your life and the intangible facets that shape your character.

Marvel at the resilience of your spirit, at your courage, and at the unwavering hope that guides your path.

Appreciate the lessons learned in times of trial, like your divorce or separation, for they have sculpted you into the person of depth and compassion that you are and you are becoming.

Extend your gratitude beyond yourself and acknowledge the people who have touched your life in immeasurable ways.

Give thanks for the caring hands that have offered solace during moments of despair, the voices that have whispered encouragement into your soul, and the kindred spirits that have stood fiercely by your side.

Each moment of gratitude becomes a bridge connecting your present to a future brimming with possibilities.

Inscribe each day's blessings upon the pages of your journal. Give birth to a collection of words that become a testament to the overflowing abundance that graces your life.

As you write, feel the energy emanating from each stroke of the pen, infusing your soul with a profound appreciation for life.

You can also be grateful in advance. Be grateful for your dreams, your hopes, and aspirations. Give thanks in anticipation of their realization.

Gratitude is the key that unlocks doors of limitless potential and invites more reasons for gratefulness into your life. So, embrace this transformative practice.

There is one more thing you need to do as part of your gratitude practice: make a promise.

Yes, a lot of us walk around with feelings of unworthiness, and when it is time to give thanks in advance for our future blessings and achievements, the ugly head of doubt creep int and generates resistance and reinforces limiting beliefs.

When you make a promise, you appease the parts of your subconscious that are spearheading the resistance, and you are neutralizing those doubts.

In other words, your promise is a bargaining tool that will help align your feelings, your intentions with your dreams; This coherence neutralizes internal conflicts within your belief system and reinforces your congruency.

Imagine that your dream is to have a big home and you give thanks in advance for this dream home. Inevitably, Then these thoughts pop up in your mind: "where is the money coming from? No one in your family has a big home! You are overreaching!

And on and on…

How does that feel?

Now, before your gratitude practice, think about what you would give in exchange. There are so many charities you could patronize, make a pledge to yourself.

Pledge, for example, to give a certain amount from now on to that charity as your way of giving thanks for your new home, NOW!

Remember, we said earlier that dreams do not come true, they are already true.

Consider the biblical definition of FAITH: the substance of things hoped for, the evidence of things not seen. (Hebrews 11:1)

Substance is matter, and in the context of faith, it refers to the tangible evidence or foundation of the things that are hoped for. Faith is the belief and confidence in something that is not yet seen or experienced.

Your pledge is a way to acknowledge receipt of what you are hoping for. You are not giving to receive; you are giving because you have already received.

Now, take a moment to think about your pledge, your promise, in thanksgiving for your dream home.

How does it feel?

Make sure you follow through on your promise. This will keep your vibration so high and will speed up your manifestation.

There is a reason tithing works. It is about giving.

The exchange here is not monetary, it is vibrational. In giving, you are matching the energy or the vibration of the thing desired, and continuously giving sustains the vibrational level until the physical manifestation of your desire.

The warmth you feel in your heart while practicing gratitude and giving is the vibrational confirmation or manifestation of your dream. It is your sign that it is on the way!

Step 6 - Audit Away

> *"Friendship is the inexpressible comfort of feeling safe with a person, having neither to weigh thoughts nor measure words."*
>
> - George Eliot

Over the years, I have lost so many friends as a direct consequence of my divorce. People I thought were friends betrayed and total strangers uplifted.

As a single mom, you need a lot of discernment in choosing friends. Be careful of the company you keep. Ensure you are with people on the same journey or people who are invested in their own growth.

It is said that some people in our lives are merely there for a season. They may be content with mediocrity, resistant to change, and uncomfortable with your transformation.

As we embark on our journey of growth, these individuals may seek to undermine our progress, consciously or not.

We must prioritize our best interests and guard ourselves against negative influences. We must be highly selective and selfish with our energy, time, and resources.

Doing so creates a shield of self-preservation that fortifies your focus.

It is time to focus.

If you are making friends, expecting they may help you, which is what friends may be for, let go of that expectation now.

Few people will truly stand in the gap for you, especially when your children are still young.

Here is an experiment for you. You can try this as a test on the people you consider friends now. Ask them to watch your kid for two hours so that you can attend to an emergency and see who responds honestly without giving you an excuse.

I know friends are not supposed to be your babysitters, but they should be able to step in and lend a helping hand or a word of comfort when you are in a bind. That is what I would do as a friend.

If none of your friends can watch your child for an hour or two, that's not friendship, that's acquaintanceship, and you should give it the level of priority it deserves.

In a world plagued by distractions and superficial connections, you must be discerning in the company we keep.

Surrounding yourself with individuals who share your aspirations and are driven towards personal growth elevates your journey.

It is crucial to shun the alluring trap of gossiping and idling because such activities drain your energy and demagnetize you.

Now is the time to realign your priorities and cultivate a magnetism towards your goals and like-minded individuals.

Seek people who inspire you to push beyond your limits and pursue greatness.

When you surround yourself with individuals who are on the same journey, you understand one another's struggles; you celebrate your victories and lend a helping hand when needed.

You become part of a community that thrives on mutual growth, and this motivates you to persist, even when faced with uncertainties.

So, audit your relationships and your friendships. Do they build you up, or do they drag you down?

Do the people you consider friends consider you their friend?

Will they do for you what you would do for them with all your responsibilities as a single mom?

Who will not be happy with your success?

Who are you afraid to leave behind if you were successful?

In my opinion, single moms must be positively selfish and strategic with their time, their resources, and their energy.

You must hold yourself accountable and consistently evaluate your actions, beliefs, and aspirations to ensure alignment with our intended trajectory.

This self-awareness allows you to remain focused, steadfast, and unwavering in becoming the best versions of yourself.

Ultimately, the company you choose to keep plays an instrumental role in shaping your destiny.

Create an environment that nurtures your potential by surrounding ourselves with individuals committed to growth.

As a single mom, you cannot afford to disperse your energy, and if you do, your children will become one of those statistics, confirming all the prejudices around single parenting and their outcomes on children.

The Path I Have Traveled

These steps helped me tremendously on my own journey. I could not be here today if I did not practice what I preach. I am retracing my steps to share with you what worked for me.

Between the book checklist in **STEP 1,** the healing sessions and the prayers, the visualization, and the gratitude practice, I developed a sense of poise and resilience that people usually comment on.

Not only did I cultivate inner strength through these practices, but I also discovered a profound connection to the world around me.

It was as if a veil had been lifted, revealing the beauty and interconnectedness that had always existed but had gone unnoticed.

With each book I delved into, I gained wisdom and perspective.

Prayer and meditation became not mere refuge but sources of strength and a way to surrender my worries and fears to a higher power with absolute trust and confidence.

Through visualizations, I learned to create my own reality, envisioning the life I desired and manifesting it.

I was able to pay for seven flight tickets, each worth over 2000 dollars, for me and my six children to move to Canada.

I recently visited my aunt, seven years later, and she said she saw me in a new light the day I boarded the plane with all my kids.

But perhaps the most transformative practice was gratitude. Not just a simple thank you, but a deep appreciation for all the blessings that surrounded me.

Through expressing gratitude daily, I cultivated a genuine sense of joy and abundance, recognizing that I had far more than I had ever realized.

But it took me years to feel whole again. I did not have **The Somatic Resonance Method**® then. I wish I did.

Implement the six steps, and you will learn the true power of a steadfast mindset.

You will uncover insights and lessons that would have taken you decades to uncover, and you will face the future with an unwavering belief in yourself and your limitless potential.

Remember, we grow through the challenges, and through our growth, we find the true beauty of life.

I became a divorce recovery coach to help other single moms move on quickly and thrive in exceptional ways.

I do not believe that time heals. I do not believe that you need to spend years in grief.

That's why I synthesized the healing methods I learned into a deep healing and fast-acting process called **The Somatic Resonance Method**®.

The Roadmap to Closure shows you the path I have traveled, so that, if you desire, you can follow my footsteps and thrive.

To your Success!

Heart Showers

The Roadmap to Closure, as outlined in this book will be enough for most single moms to spring back to action and thrive.

However, if you need more guidance to heal your heart, which is a deepening of STEP 2, this part of the book is for you.

As you can imagine, "cleaning the house" can be challenging for a lot of single moms, because our emotions can have a mind of their own.

Healing your heart can be a journey in itself, but thankfully, there are tools to help you transmute the pain and convert it into power.

My next book is titled **Closure Challenge: From Heartbreak To Radiance In 33 Days,** and it gives your heat a good shower.

If you have ever asked *"how do I get my memories not to bother me anymore?"* this book is your answer.

It combines deep insights into divorce healing journey with powerful Somatic Resonance healing sessions that target specific issues and associated emotions and bring you release and freedom almost instantaneously.

It is a practical book that goes straight to the point. No clichés, no empty platitudes!

See the Table of contents below.

The Closure Challenge: From Heartbreak To Radiance In 33 Days

TABLE OF CONTENTS

PART I

Copyright
Dedication
Foreword
Goals and Expectations
Core Healing Principles
The SRM of Healing
Warning: How to Use This Book
Materials Needed
Flow of the Challenge
Bonus – Procrastination Healing Session
The Feeling of Healing

PART II

Day 1 - Landmark Dates and Anniversaries (Addressing Regret, Guilt Anger)

Day 2 - Clothing - Wedding Clothes and Memorabilia (Addressing Anger)

Day 3 - Gifts, Wedding Gifts and Mementos (Addressing Resentment)

Day 4 - Wedding Bands and Symbolic Jewelry (Addressing Jealousy)

Day 5 - Pictures and Photo Triggers (Addressing Longing)

Day 6 - Names and Terms of Endearment (Addressing Longing, regrets, anger)

Day 7 - Intimacy and Body image, body Triggers (Addressing Self-Worth)

Day 8 - Memories of Pregnancies

Day 9 - Children (Addressing Guilt)

Day 10 - Anniversaries and Birthdays (Addressing Loneliness)

Day 11 - Shame and Self-Blame (Addressing Self-Acceptance)

Day 12 - Loss of the Family Unit (Addressing Grief)

Day 13 - Pets (Addressing Sadness)

Day 14 - Shared Properties (cars, Houses) (Addressing Loss)

Day 15 - Marital Status (regrets, Resentment)

Day 16 - Favorite Places Visited Together/planned on Visiting Together (Addressing Nostalgia)

Day 17 - Acts of Love (Tattoos, Gifts) (embarrassment; Regret/Shame)

Day 18 - Projects and Dreams (Addressing Disappointment)

Day 19 - Personal Triggers and Amplifiers (upbringing, Experience)

Day 20 - Broken Promises and Agreements

Day 21 - Common Couple and Family Routines

Day 22 - What Ifs

Day 23 - Loss Time and Starting Over

Day 24 - In-Laws (Addressing Resentment)

Day 25 - Mutual Friends, Ex Friends and in Between (Addressing Isolation)

Day 26 - Co-Parenting Challenges (Addressing Frustration)

Day 27 - New Girlfriends/boyfriends (jealousy, Resentment)

Day 28 - New Dreams and Goals (Addressing Hope, Frustration)

Part III

Workbook

About The Author

Clairine, The Closure Coach, is a single mom of six amazing children, and she has a soft spot for single moms around the world.

Her goal is to help them piece their hearts back together, use their history as fuel for the next chapter of their lives, and thrive.

She sought training to be able to achieve this goal and for two other reasons.

First, she saw single moms' pain and suffering in chat groups over the years, and it increasingly pained her that no concrete solutions were being offered.

She belonged to many online single moms' groups, and her heart ached when she read posts expressing pain, anger, resentment, frustration. She knew she could help but she had no formal coaching training.

She was even more motivated when she got banned from two groups because she often offered a different perspective and people increasingly tagged her on posts to have her opinion. Admins did not like it.

The other group banned her because she made a statement about the so-called "absentee fathers" that did not sit right with the admins.

In essence, she said the "*absentee father*" concept is a lie, and she gave my reasons.

It created a huge debate, and before the admins stepped in and deleted the post, she had received dozens of messages thanking her for her insights and a few enraged ones.

The second reason is that she has been there, and for some amazing reason, she was self-aware enough to keep tabs on what she did that was working for her, and over the years, she has retraced her steps and helped hundreds of single moms.

For the past six years, she has been taking courses, certifications, reading books, and attending seminars to work on her own lingering issues and to streamline her coaching process around the question: *"How does one find closure?"*

She has tested and tweaked this process until she could narrow it down to my Somatic Resonance Method and the six steps outlined in this book.

In a final twist of destiny, she had to taste my own medicine when she dipped her toes in the dating pool again last year.

She is a certified Coach and holds several certifications and took many courses and attended numerous seminars for different modalities to resolve traumas and help people find peace.

So, she has an extensive toolbox. Here are just a few of her tools:

Neurolinguistic Programming (NLP) or how to leverage the power of our words, our voice, our thoughts on your neurology for a better life). (NLP Power)

The Silva Method-ESP or how to tap into the subconscious mind and problem-solve for yourself and for other people.

Practitioners of the Silva Method learn to achieve deeper levels of consciousness to access their inner potential, manage stress, improve learning capabilities, and achieve their goals through mental reprogramming. (Avlis, MindValley, SilvaESP)

Cognitive Behavioral Therapy (CBT), or how to be alert and aware to change any behavior you don't like. (Coaching Studies Academy)

Emotional Freedom Technique (RFT), or how to talk to your body to release any negative emotions.

MAP (Make Anything Possible), or how to marry the power of your Superconscious with your imagination to heal traumas painlessly, access inner alignment and unveil your life's purpose. Etc. (The MAP Coaching Institute)

True Purpose, or how to give yourself permission to succeed and thrive. (The True Purpose Institute)

Quantum Healing Method (QHM), or how to facilitate deep states of relaxation and altered consciousness in clients, allowing them to access their past lives, explore their higher selves, and gain insights into their current life challenges and purposes. (Harper Healing)

Sacred Body Language Translation (SBLT), or how to interpret unconscious gestures people make, because every single one of those gestures tells a profound story about the person. (Mastery Systems)

Imagination Activation (IA), or how to leverage the power of your imagination and the power of your subconscious mind to shape the life you desire because your imagination is your access door to God's laboratory. (Mastery Systems)

Bio-Optic Holography (BoH), or what your eyes say about your lineage, your life now and your future, and how to address generational issues they point to. (Mastery Systems)

Medical Chinese Face reading (MCFR) - or how to read someone's face, detect past traumas and help them resolve them, detect future potential traumas, and help them avert them. (NLP Power)

And, her signature healing process, **The Somatic Resonance Method (SRM)**, where she combines different elements of these modalities for a greater and more focused impact on divorce wounds.

In another life, Clairine is a professional French translator (M.A.), French being her first language, and she is currently pursuing a PhD in Metaphysical Counselling.

Resources

<u>Join Our Facebook Community</u>

Remember, healing is not a solitary pursuit. It is essential to seek support and to surround yourself with people on the same journey of growth.

Click here to join Our Facebook community or search Closure Solutions on Facebook.

Contact Us: <u>info@closuresolutions.org</u>

<u>Book updates</u>

Sign up here or go to https://clairine-yomi.formaloo.me/i0uxv if you would like to receive updates about my next book (Find the Table Of Contents Below).

<u>Click here</u> to visit my links or go to <u>https://sleekbio.com/theclosurecoach</u>

www.ingramcontent.com/pod-product-compliance
Lightning Source LLC
Chambersburg PA
CBHW022056050726
47591CB00002B/575